MANIFEST *your* FUTURE

A GUIDE FOR
THE MODERN MYSTIC

This edition published in 2022
By SJG Publishing, HP22 6NF, UK

Author: Helen Vaux
Design: Blackbird Brands
Illustrations under licence from Shutterstock.com
Additional illustrations by Nick Pettit

ISBN: 978-1-913004-60-6

Printed in China

10 9 8 7 6 5 4 3 2 1

CONTENTS

"The future belongs to those who believe in the beauty of their dreams."

Eleanor Roosevelt

INTRODUCTION

. . . .

Do you ever feel like you're living life on autopilot, being swept along on a wave? Does it feel like things happen to you? That you have no control over your destiny? You can change this. You have the power to shape your own life and achieve the goals you've always dreamed of. What's more, it's a wonderful journey full of self-love that will show you what an amazing person you are.

"But I'm not a mystic!"

Well, maybe not in a traditional sense, but the fact you've even picked up this book means you're someone who is open to the idea there are hidden realities beyond what we perceive with our senses. The 'modern mystic' understands the importance of physical, mental and spiritual harmony. They seek out practices and beliefs that help achieve that internal equilibrium.

This book will guide you on a journey of transformation where you'll discover how to use your spirit and your energy to create ('manifest') the future you want using the 'law of attraction'. Everything in the book you can do in your own home or environment.

Remember, the universe has plans for you and they are already manifesting, fuelled by your own desires and intentions. All you need to do is open your heart and mind – and believe …

AM I A MYSTIC?

. . . .

'Mystic' is a loosely defined term so it's no wonder you're not sure whether you can call yourself one! Whilst you might not be casting spells or telling fortunes, below are ten signs you are almost certainly on a mystical wavelength.

- ☀ You ponder existence. Why am I here? What is my purpose?
- ☀ You trust your intuition and listen to the universe.
- ☀ You believe in personal growth and nurturing your inner self.
- ☀ You accept that the universe is mysterious – and that you certainly don't know everything!
- ☀ You acknowledge that love is a powerful energy connecting the universe.
- ☀ Your wisdom is your own and you arrive at it through your personal experiences and intuition.
- ☀ You enjoy being alone and can use it as a time for reflection and introspection. You find it easy to separate yourself from the 'real world'.
- ☀ You live in the present – the past and future don't truly exist.
- ☀ You embrace change as it brings opportunities and growth.
- ☀ You gain validation from within, not from others or by conforming to social norms.

the
basic
principles

In this section of the book, you'll discover more about the principles of manifestation and the law of attraction. With this knowledge, you'll have a greater understanding of how and why manifestation works and the ideal mindset to adopt to make wonderful things happen.

WHAT IS MANIFESTATION?

....

MANIFEST-OH! Manifestation isn't magic. It involves
visualizing what you want in life and channelling your
energy and actions to make it happen. It uses your thoughts,
intentions and the energies in the universe to change your
life and turn dreams into reality. A powerful tool, indeed!

The power of energy

Everything in the universe is made up of energy. This means that nothing
is constant or fixed – therefore, in theory, we can shape our own inner
and outer realities. (We can thank Albert Einstein for this observation
and for connecting physics with philosophy!)

Thanks to energy, the world is in vibration. Even though your energy
vibrates on its own individual frequency, everything in the universe is
connected. Once we understand that, we can tune into the frequencies
around us, harness energy and manifest (create and shape) the future.

Our thoughts create tiny sparks of energy in our brains and these vibrate
at a certain frequency. The frequency of these 'thought vibrations'
communicates with your cells, which, in turn, send out electromagnetic
waves with the same frequency as the original thought. The more belief
you have in those thoughts, the more powerful the waves you send
out to the universe. (Interestingly, our hearts send out the strongest
electromagnetic waves.) It's pretty mind-boggling! Even scientists
don't know quite how we do this.

The law of attraction

Central to manifestation is 'the law of attraction'. This is the idea that 'like attracts like'. So, positive energy attracts positive energy and, on the flipside, negative attracts negative. If you can use your positivity to create equally positive energy in the world around you, good things will happen. We're all human though and constant positive thinking simply isn't sustainable. However, what we can do is learn to tune into our thoughts and intervene when we detect unhelpful thinking that creates an obstacle to the future we want (for more on this, turn to page 13).

The law of attraction is what makes manifestation possible. The universe will provide you with what you desire if you put the work in to attract those outcomes. Key to manifestation is realising that action is just as vital as your thoughts. And it isn't a quick solution. It takes time and effort … and patience!

Think …

Have you met someone who wasn't 'on your wavelength'? You didn't really hit it off and it felt like you had nothing in common. If your energy levels were on a different frequency – not on the same wavelength – you won't be in harmony with each other. Universal energy and the law of attraction are very real, even if you don't realize it at the time!

How to make energy work for you

Universal energy and the law of attraction are all well and good, but how do we use them to consciously create and manifest the future? We know the tools, but what do we do with them? For a mystical concept that's hard to get your head around, manifestation requires a surprisingly practical approach (combined with plenty of trust in yourself and the universe). Thankfully, this is what this book is all about. For the time being, sit tight and feel the following tips:

Be in the right frame of mind

- Be clear in your vision and what you want to achieve.
- Believe in your power to align with the power of the universe.
- Aspire to match the vibrations of the results you want to attract.
- Embrace gratitude.
- Immerse yourself in feeling – we attract what we feel.
- Think, act and feel like your dreams are already a reality.
- Take daily intentional actions to achieve your goals – they won't happen by themselves!
- Don't doubt that you are the creator of your future!

"The true mystic is always both humble and compassionate, for she knows that she does not know."

Richard Rohr

GETTING STARTED

. . . .

MANIFEST-OH! Your 'intent' is your soul's deepest desires.
It could be the type of person you want to be (loving, loved,
compassionate) or an outcome you want to achieve (to be
successful in your chosen career). Intent is spiritual and
emotional and it forms the basis for your manifestations.

Questions, questions, questions!

Some people go through life not really questioning who they really are or what their purpose in life is – and that's okay. Modern mystics, however, ponder their existence and their place in the universe, knowing that they might not always find the right answer, or even any answer at all. If you look deep inside yourself and contemplate what you want from life, you will uncover your intent. Start by asking yourself these questions (and the further questions they inevitably give rise to!):

Who am I?
Who do you want to be? How do you want to feel? What do you want to give back to the universe? Can you integrate spiritual knowledge and self-knowledge into your world so that you live a more conscious and fuller life?

What do I want?
What specific goals do you want to achieve in life (particularly if money were no object)? What do you want to manifest? It could be a career ambition, a grade level for the instrument you play, to get married, to take a year out to go travelling . . . Provided your goal is realistic, the possibilities are endless!

Understanding who you are and what you want from life is a wonderful journey of exploration. The path might be winding, but you will learn to be flexible and resilient.

Goal setting

Goals are task-oriented and have an end result. It is important that your intent sits behind your goals. Your intent helps you immerse yourself in the feeling of what you want to achieve. Remember the 'law of attraction' (page 9) – we attract what we feel. Writing your goals down makes you more likely to achieve them. Having a plan gives you a direction, which in turn improves your resilience and wellbeing and reduces worry. Setting goals provides short- and long-term motivation and helps you focus on what you need to do – internally and externally – to get there.

Tips for successful goalsetting

- Make sure your goal is realistic and achievable – if you're 85, you're never going to be a commercial jet pilot!

- Make your goal specific rather than vague. Plan out the specific actions you need to take – and be prepared for that plan to change.

- Commit to your goal. Writing it down is a good starting point. And BELIEVE in it.

- Visualizing your goal will help motivate you and boost your confidence. See page 38.

- Always be kind to yourself. Be prepared for setbacks, learn from them and move on.

WHAT'S STOPPING YOU?

. . . .

MANIFEST-OH! Whatever the size of your goal or dream, you'll find excuses to put it off if you're feeling daunted. It's natural to feel this way, particularly if it's something you're passionate about achieving but you fear failure. Overcoming these obstacles is all part of the journey.

The fear factor

Even the most intrepid of modern mystics worry – we're all human. If we didn't fret a little, we wouldn't think ahead to mitigate risk or have contingency plans up our sleeves. Whilst you must trust the universe, successful manifestation isn't about just wishing for something and waiting for it to happen – you must play an active role. But what if fear is holding you back? Start by making a list of what could go wrong and then follow these steps:

- On a scale of 1–10, how real are those risks? Are you imagining obstacles that aren't there?

- If the risks are real, what can you do to limit them? (e.g. enlist a friend for support, have a back-up plan.)

- Think about how you'd feel if those obstacles weren't an issue. Excited? Confident? Powerful?

> *"'What if I fall?' Oh but my darling, What if you fly?"*
>
> Erin Hanson

13

Tell the right people

Telling your nearest and dearest about your goals is a big step. What was once only in your head is suddenly out in the open for all to see. There is evidence to suggest that telling people can help you achieve your goals as it reinforces your commitment to success. However, vocalizing your dreams can see them struck down: "Are you mad?", "Don't be ridiculous!", "You're too old!". So, if you do share your dreams, only share them with those who are on your wavelength. The last thing you want is nay-sayers chipping away at your self-belief.

Tips to boost your self-belief

To manifest your future, you must believe in yourself and trust in the universe.

- **Don't compare yourself to others.** Life isn't a competition — you have your own strengths, passions and dreams so focus on those, not on other people.

- **Surround yourself with positive people** who love you and want the best for you.

- **Practice self-care.** When you're doing something positive for your mind, body and soul, you will naturally feel more confident. (See page 32 for more about self-care.)

- **Be kind to yourself.** (Read more about self-love on page 31.)

- **Remember:** Setbacks aren't failures — they help you learn and grow and are all part of the workings of the universe. Reset, readjust and move on.

A WORD OF CAUTION

You can work in harmony with the universe to consciously create your future, but it isn't magic. Things won't happen just because you want them to. You need to combine your spiritual intent with practical, everyday work – *actions*.

The techniques in this book will give you the extra 'oomph' to achieve your goals, but they don't replace good old-fashioned hard work.

For example ...

... you desperately want to work for a particular company. Your experience and qualifications are perfectly suited. So, you create a vision board, position your crystals carefully and meditate – but a year later you're still no closer to working at the company. If you don't physically apply for an advertised role or send a speculative letter, your dream of working at the company won't come true!

It is also worth noting that none of the techniques and suggestions in this book are intended to replace medical opinion. If you have concerns about your health – physical, emotional and mental – always seek professional advice.

So, with that in mind, it's time to delve into the practices and techniques that modern mystics like you need to manifest the life and the future you want ....

"The whole universe is working in your favor. The universe has got your back!"

Ralph Smart

tools and techniques

Here, we move on to the tools and techniques a modern mystic can use to support manifestation. They will open your heart, soul and mind to infinite possibilities, allowing you to project your own positive energy and attract and receive the energies of the universe around you. It's as good as it sounds!

SPIRITUAL BATHING

. . . .

*MANIFEST-OH! A relaxing bath has always been a tonic
to the stresses and strains of everyday life. But it can be
much more than that, especially when you consciously
make it a spiritual experience. Spiritual bathing is
soaking in the tub on another level.*

What is spiritual bathing?

Spiritual bathing is far more than running a hot bath, filling it with bubbles
and pouring yourself a glass of wine – although that's good for you too.
It's an ancient practice that has long been part of healing traditions around
the world. A spiritual bath reconnects you to your soul and washes away
the obstacles that might be stopping you from living a full, conscious life.

But how does it work? Spiritual bathing uses water's vibrational energy
along with natural elements (such as plants and flowers) to cleanse you.
It creates the space you need to see both your inner self and the outer
world with clarity.

The benefits

Spiritual bathing has many positive benefits. It will:

- Uplift your spirit.
- Increase your confidence.
- Lower stress and anxiety.

- Release you from fear.
- Help you feel less overwhelmed.

These benefits ensure you're in the right frame of mind to manifest your dreams and desires. After a spiritual bath you'll be more receptive to your inner voice and better able to tune into the energy of the universe around you.

Now dip your toe in . . .

Unless you know an expert in spiritual bathing, enjoy making this an entirely homemade experience.

1. Prepare by making sure the space where you will take your bath is clean and decluttered. Pay special attention to corners as this is where stagnant energy tends to collect.

2. Fill your bath, ensuring the water temperature is comfortable. You can add anything around the bathroom that you feel would help you relax, for example candles, incense or crystals. Turn down the lights or play soothing music.

3. Add the appropriate ingredients to your bath. (See Magic Ingredients on the next page.) Then, stir the bath water – anti-clockwise if your intention is to take something away (e.g. negative energy) or clockwise if your intention is to attract something (e.g. love). Whether the direction really makes a difference or not, feel the energy that you're giving to the water by stirring it. And it's perfectly fine for the modern mystic to use their hand if a wand isn't available!

4. When you feel the moment is right, submerge yourself in the bath. Ensure your body is covered by the water and gently pour some over your head.

5. Whilst relaxing in the bath, imagine you are being cleansed and that any negativity is being washed away. Meditate (see page 66), acknowledge any thoughts that come into your head but let them pass like clouds, especially if they are negative thoughts. Visualize achieving your dream or goal and focus on how it makes you feel. Perhaps you're feeling enveloped in love or a huge sense of achievement after getting the promotion you want.

6. When you're ready (and before the water gets too chilly), get out of the bath and let yourself drip dry. You should now feel wonderfully relaxed, rejuvenated and clear-headed. Plus, you'll be full of the positivity that you need to attract positive energy into your life.

Magic ingredients

There's a huge list of plants and herbs that you can add to your spiritual bath. The trick is to match the ingredient to what it is you're trying to manifest. Here are a few ideas, but you can use the modern mystic's favourite tool (the internet!) to discover more:

- **To attract money:**
  almond, basil, chamomile, ginger, jasmine, marjoram, mint, pine.

- **To attract love:**
  aloe, hemp, hibiscus, lavender, pear, peppermint, rosemary, vanilla.

- **To cleanse your energy:**
  blueberry, coconut, lavender, parsley, peppermint, thyme.

- **For peace:**
  lavender, passionflower, violet.

The easiest way to add these ingredients to your bath is to put them in a muslin bag and let them brew in the bath – just like you're making a huge cup of tea. Alternatively, place them in a heatproof jar and cover with boiling water, cover the top of the jar and leave to infuse until the water has cooled. Then simply strain the water to remove the leaves, etc., and add the liquid to your bath. And if you don't have fresh ingredients to hand, you can use essential oils instead.

A LITTLE WORD OF WARNING

Always, always check you're not allergic to any of the ingredients or oils you add to your bath. If you're not sure, rub it on a small patch of skin and leave for 24 hours to see if you have a reaction. Only use ingredients that you are 100% sure are safe.

Moon bathing

If you enjoy spiritual bathing, give moon bathing a try. The energy of the moon is believed to help you relax and trust in the universe to take charge. A full moon signifies the height of positive mental energy and empowers you to be grateful for all you have and all you want to achieve. Moon bathing therefore helps you acquire the mindset needed for making manifestation work. There are two ways to moon bathe:

1. Sit, lay down or take a walk beneath the light of the full moon. (You can keep your clothes on!) Visualize your intentions and feel how you are soaking up the moon's transformational energy.

2. Create a moon water bath. Place a bowl of water in the moonlight for no less than an hour to infuse it with the moon's energy. Then simply pour it into a full bathtub and enjoy the soak. Cleansing yourself with moon water can amplify your intentions and increase the power of manifestation.

After a moon bath, you will feel full of positive energy.

Use the new moon

A new moon bath – when the least amount of moonlight is reaching the earth – is an ideal time to set your intentions for what you want to manifest.

UNBLOCK YOUR CHAKRAS

. . . .

MANIFEST–OH! If you don't already know about your chakras, they're fascinating. Understanding and cleansing your chakras is an important part of manifesting a happier, more abundant life.

What is a chakra?

The easiest way to think of a chakra is as point of energy in your body. You have seven chakras and they work together to generate your life force and regulate the flow of energy through your whole body. It's essential that your chakras are balanced to create harmony of mind, body and spirit.

Your seven chakras

Your chakras sit along an energy line that runs from the top of your head to the base of your spine. Each one has a specific meaning and purpose and relates to a different part of your body.

CROWN CHAKRA
Located at the top of your head, this chakra is your centre of consciousness and spiritual connectedness. It relates to understanding, bliss, purpose and personal destiny. A balanced crown chakra brings enlightenment!
Chakra colour: violet.
Body: cerebral cortex, nervous system and pituitary gland.
Element: inner light.

Crown chakra
Third eye chakra
Throat chakra
Heart chakra
Solar plexus chakra
Sacral chakra
Root chakra

THIRD EYE CHAKRA

Located at the centre of your forehead, slightly above eye level. This chakra relates to questions, perception, knowing, inner vision, intuition and wisdom. Your personal dreams for life are situated in this chakra.
Chakra colour: indigo.
Body: eyes, brain, nervous system, pineal gland.
Element: light.

THROAT CHAKRA

Located within your throat, this chakra relates to communication, creativity, self-expression, judgement, healing, intuition, purpose, sense of timing and transformation.
Chakra colour: blue/turquoise.
Body: neck, shoulders, arms, hands, thyroid.
Element: ether.

HEART CHAKRA
Located in your heart (of course!), this chakra relates to love, compassion, harmony and peace.
Chakra colour: green.
Body: lungs, heart, arms, hands, thymus gland.
Element: air.

SOLAR PLEXUS CHAKRA
Located a few inches above your navel, at your solar plexus. This chakra relates to emotions, including laughter, happiness and anger, and your ambition.
Chakra colour: yellow.
Body: digestive system, muscles, pancreas, adrenals.
Element: fire.

SACRAL CHAKRA
Located between the base of your spine and your navel, this chakra relates to pleasure, sexuality, reproduction and creativity.
Chakra colour: orange.
Body: kidneys, bladder, circulatory system, reproductive organs and glands.
Element: water.

ROOT CHAKRA
Located at the base of your spine, this chakra controls your fight or flight response and how grounded you are.
Chakra colour: red.
Body: legs, feet, bones, large intestine, adrenal glands.
Element: earth.

Blocked chakras

When your chakras are blocked it can disrupt your spiritual harmony and your physical wellbeing. For example, a blocked throat chakra can manifest itself as dishonesty and lack of creativity. A blocked root chakra might result in a heightened sense of fear and anxiety. When your chakras aren't functioning, the flow of energy around your body is interrupted.

What can cause blockages?

- Stress
- Grief
- Illness
- Poor diet
- Fear
- Denial
- Suppressed emotions … the list could go on!

So, how do you know if your chakras need attention? Well, if all is working well, you'll have a feeling of contentment and wellbeing. If you don't and are feeling stressed, drained, unwell or rundown, there's a good chance you have a blockage somewhere. Time to fix it!

Chakra cleansing

It's not always possible to identify where your blockage is. The best thing to do is start from your root chakra and work your way up. Cleansing your chakras will get the positive energy re-flowing around your body so that you feel like the best version of yourself again. Here are some ways to tackle your blockages:

1. Reconnect with the elements. Each chakra is associated with an element (see previous pages) – reconnecting with that element will cleanse the chakra and put you back on the path to equilibrium. For example, if your sacral chakra (water) needs work, go swimming or listen to the ocean; if your third eye chakra (light) needs replenishing, spend a day outside in the sunshine. See the Connect to the Earth chapter (see page 53) for more ways to earth yourself.

2. Crystals can clear or enhance your energy. Choose your crystals based on the blocked chakra. For more about how modern mystics can harness the power of crystals, see page 34.

3. Your chakras all have an associated colour. Surrounding yourself with that colour (home décor, clothes), gazing at the colour and even eating food of that colour can help cleanse your chakra. Consider it colour therapy! It's not a cure-all but it is fun.

4. Meditation is a brilliant way to clear your chakras and get back on an even keel. (Try a chakra meditation, page 68).

5. Affirmations are more than just feel-good quotes. They have the power to reprogramme your brain, rebalance chakras and put you in a mindset where you're more likely to achieve your goals. (See page 29 for more on affirmations.)

6. Specific types of yoga can unblock your chakras. If you've practised yoga, you'll have noticed the connection between chakras and 'heart opening' poses, for example. Delve a little deeper on page 78.

7. Reiki. This would require a Guide for the Modern Mystic all of its own! If you're interested in this form of healing to channel and direct energy into your blocked chakras, it's recommended that you seek out a reiki master.

OPEN THE DOOR: AFFIRMATIONS

· ·

MANIFEST–OH! Positive affirmations can the open door to new opportunities and set you on a path to change. Believing in yourself and what you can achieve is a vital part of manifestation. The greater your belief in your goals, the more positive energy you will attract. That's when thing start to happen.

What is an affirmation?

When you affirm something, you give your support to it. A positive affirmation has the power to uplift you and provide the confidence and courage you need to take control of your future. For example: "I can create the future I want." Or something more specific: "I can start my own dog grooming business." The most effective affirmations:

- use the present tense – "I am", "I can".
- use positive words – "I will" rather than "I won't".
- are firm, so no wishy-washy words like "I could" or "I'd like to".

How do affirmations work?

As much as we like to think of ourselves as complex beings, our brains are quite simple. They like clear instructions that are easy to process and store. For an affirmation to stick in your brain (and for your brain to start doing its clever work with it), you need to repeat the affirmation. Every time your brain hears the affirmation, it will strengthen the positive connection.

Write your affirmations on post-it notes and stick them around your home; set aside 5 minutes every morning and evening to say your affirmations in front of a mirror – do whatever works for you, but do it often. You can also use affirmations as part of meditation to boost their impact (see page 70).

Feeling the statement is important. Only then will you start to believe it in both your heart and your head. Where negative thoughts and doubts previously popped into your head, they will gradually be replaced by positive thoughts. And as we know, projecting positive energy brings all the good stuff right back to us.

Ten great affirmations for manifesting

I deserve to be happy and successful.

I welcome new opportunities and change.

I attract prosperity into my life.

I am on the path to achieving my goals.

The universe loves and supports me.

I let go of all fears and doubts that hold me back.

I am grateful for all I have.

I am a powerful individual.

I use my energy to create the life I want.

Every day, I make the conscious effort to make my life even better.

LOVE YOURSELF

. . . .

*MANIFEST–OH! Being told that you 'love yourself'
can be a criticism. It suggests you're overly confident
or self-centred. But it's a positive thing!
Loving ourselves – self-love – is essential for inner
peace and accepting who we are so that we can
channel that strength into manifesting our dreams.*

What does it really mean to love yourself?

- You accept your strengths and weaknesses.

- You listen to and trust your intuition (that 'gut feeling').

- You rise above the judgement of others.

- You listen to your body – the aches and pains, the twinges. You know when it is trying to tell you to slow down or do things differently. You appreciate how amazing your body is.

- You know that you don't always get things right, but you're willing to reflect on events and learn how you could have managed them better or differently. You want to grow.

- **YOU ARE KIND TO YOURSELF.**

Self-love helps you understand WHO you are, WHAT your values are and WHY you behave in a particular way. Without this clarity, it is harder to see the bigger picture and design the future you want to manifest.

How to practice self-love

Self-love is about the introspection that helps you grow as a person. It is also about simple acts of self-care that improve our mood and bring joy. The relationship you have with yourself is crucial to your wellbeing and for creating healthy and happy relationships in the world around you. If you're new to showing yourself love – and, let's face it, most people are accomplished self-critics – then start with these basic principles:

Know when to say 'no' … and when to say 'yes'

Set boundaries in your life. It's okay to say 'no' to something that your intuition says isn't right for you. And don't feel guilty for saying 'no'. Ask yourself whether something (or someone) has a positive part to play in the future you want to manifest.

On the flipside, know when to say 'yes' to something you're not entirely sure about. It could well be the universe sending something your way – you never know, exciting opportunities might arise out of it. Go with your gut feeling.

Accept what is happening in your life

We all have good days and bad days. It's hard not to be knocked off kilter by the latter. But modern mystics go with the flow. They trust in the universe, believing that things happen for a reason. Rather than beating yourself up when things aren't going well, ask yourself: "What is the universe trying to tell me? What can I learn from this?" The future you were trying to manifest might need a slight tweak. After all, life isn't a straight road so be prepared for twists and turns. Rest assured that you'll get to your destination eventually – and if it looks different to the destination you originally had in mind, it will still be the right one for you.

Don't compare yourself to others

Modern mystics believe in personal growth and nurturing their inner self. How does comparing yourself to others help with that? The answer is it doesn't. Everyone is treading a different path so what's right for someone else might not be right for you. Focus on manifesting your own best life – living someone else's dream is not the route to self-fulfilment.

Do something that you love – every day

Make sure you set aside 'me time' to do things that make you happy. Dance to your favourite record, take a spiritual bath (see page 18), read a book sitting in the sun, eat a sausage roll fresh from the oven. Whatever it is, no matter how big or small, do it. It will recharge your energy levels. When your energy is firing on all cylinders, that's when you'll be shooting out all those good vibes around the universe, encouraging manifestation.

Get more sleep

Don't underestimate the power of a good night's sleep. Not only will it recharge your batteries, but it lets you digest everything from that day. Whilst you sleep, new learning and experiences are filed in the amazing storage cabinet that is your brain. You'll wake up looking the same (well, perhaps with a rested glow!), but inside you'll have grown.

Digital detox

Ask yourself what social media contributes to the goals you're aiming for. It steals time where you could be doing something more spiritually enriching and lowers self-esteem (why haven't you got an Insta-perfect life?!). Take the plunge and give social media a break for a couple of days. You'll soon see positive benefits.

THE POWER OF CRYSTALS

* *

*MANIFEST-OH! All good mystics accept that the universe is
a mysterious place and sometimes we must trust in things
we struggle to understand. For some people, crystals are one
of those things. Open your mind and read on to discover the
role crystals can play in manifestation.*

More than just a chunk of rock

Crystals have been used for their special energies since the year dot.
But how do they work? It is believed that the minerals found in crystals
create a vibration that attracts other energies into your life. (Remember
the law of attraction? See page 9.) They can also help you send your own
vibrations out into the universe. Depending on which crystal you use, the
vibrations of that crystal can be used to manifest different outcomes.

Choosing your crystals

To cover the uses of every crystal would require an encyclopaedia for the modern mystic, not a short guide. Crystals come in all shapes and sizes and each has its own particular special qualities.

Below is a selection of crystals believed to be most beneficial to manifestation (those in bold are particularly linked to that energy focus).

CRYSTAL	ENERGY FOCUS	ASSOCIATED CHAKRA
Black Tourmaline	Protection, absorbs negative energy	Root
Rose quartz	**Love, dreams**	Heart
Amethyst	Wisdom, **spirituality**, clarity, **health, dreams**	Crown
Agate	Balance, harmony	All
Carnelian	Creativity, determination, vitality, **love**	Sacral
Hematite	Focus, grounding to the earth	Root
Moonstone	Intuition, femininity	Crown
Pyrite	Wealth	Solar plexus
Tiger's eye	**Success**, insight, intuition, **personal power**	Third Eye
Clear quartz	Anything and everything!	All
Aventurine	Luck, abundance, self-confidence, creativity, money, prosperity, health	Heart
Citrine	**Abundance, money**, prosperity, joy, **creativity, careers**	Solar plexus
Rhodonite	Love, self love	Heart
Kunzite	Unconditional **love**, self-love	Heart
Garnet	**Personal power**, courage and good health	Root
Black obsidian	Health, protection from negative energy, ability to see the truth	Root

How to use your crystals

There are numerous ways to tap into the natural energy of crystals.
All the methods attract a crystal's positive energy into your life and focus
your mind on the outcome you're trying to create.

Start by choosing a crystal (or crystals) that connects to what you want
to manifest. Then, set a clear intention of what you want to achieve
with the crystal – for example, "I want to bring courage into my life."

- **Place crystals around your home.** You can go into great depth on the
  placement of crystals, such as putting them in specific places or in a
  grid arrangement. For example, carnelian in the bedroom could boost
  your sex life and black tourmaline in the entry hall protects against
  negative energy coming through the front door. However, simply
  placing them in the corners of your living areas is just as effective.
  Try not to hide them away – you need to be conscious that they're
  there, not forget them and leave them gathering dust!

- **Meditate with your crystals.** Hold the crystal in your hand (or have
  it nearby) as you meditate on your intentions. See page 66 for more
  about using meditation for manifestation.

- **Wear them!** Bracelets, necklaces, tucked in your pocket, in your
  bag – there are many ways to keep your crystals right at your side.

Be patient, you might not see an immediate effect. Because crystals
have a natural energy, they can start working in just a few days. However,
they may take months. It depends on you too – how much effort are you
putting into creating positive energy?

Unblock your chakras with crystals

As we know from the chapter on chakras (see page 24), if your chakras are blocked, the flow of energy around your body is disturbed. This isn't unhelpful when you're relying on your energy for successful manifestation. Crystals can be used to clear or enhance your energy by cleansing the chakras that are blocked. Choose your crystals based on where the blockage is (see the table on page 35 for ideas).

To unblock your chakras using crystals, you can use the suggestions described previously in 'How to use your crystals'. You can also try relaxing (sitting or lying down) with a crystal placed on the corresponding chakra point. If you're meditating, visualizing the colour of the chakra you are focusing on can make the cleansing effect even more powerful.

Recharge your crystals

Your crystals will have a stronger energy and work better for manifestation if your cleanse and recharge them regularly. Rest assured, this doesn't involve any naked incantations!

Use these methods instead:

- Put your crystals in a dish and leave them in direct sunlight for a few hours. Moonlight also works.

- Wash them under running water and dry them on a towel.

- Holding the crystal while you meditate can also recharge them with your own energy. Focus on the crystal and visualize filling it with light and power.

VISUALIZATION: ALL IN THE MIND

. . . .

MANIFEST-OH! Manifestation needs you to believe in the future you want to create. You must see it and feel it – even touch it and taste it if that's what it takes! One of the most effective ways to do this is through visualization. Being able to visualize success has been shown to increase your chances of achieving what you want.

Make your brain work for you

Pablo Picasso once said, "Everything you can imagine is real." He was right – your brain doesn't know the difference between reality and imagination. Whilst that might sound like a weakness, it's actually a strength as it means we can trick our minds into believing in something that hasn't yet happened. Perfect for when you want to manifest your future.

It's straightforward: focus on positive visualizations and you can shape the life you want. Of course, it doesn't guarantee something is going to happen. As with all the techniques in this book, it's not magic – and you're a mystic not a magician. What visualization gives you is belief in yourself and confidence that the future you want is real and achievable.

"When you visualize, then you materialize."
Denis Waitley

Visualize success

Creating a visualization isn't complicated and, with a bit of imagination, can be great fun. Here is a simple but effective visualization technique:

1. Make yourself comfortable, but stay upright! Calm your mind by taking five slow, deep breaths. Breathe in to the count of five and out to five.

2. Think of your goal or the change you want to happen in your life. It could be small (getting a cat) or big (starting a new business).

3. Time to activate your senses! Visualize what your goal looks like when it's successful – be in it and feel yourself living it. Make it feel real. How does it make you feel to have achieved your goal?

4. Visualize the scene in as much detail as possible. For example, if you're focusing on a new retail business, imagine yourself in your shop. What does it look like? What are you wearing? What are the customers doing? Breathe deeply and enjoy how good it feels. Hold this feeling.

5. You can also add an affirmation to your visualization. In the example above, you could say to yourself, "I am running a successful business". Simply nodding your head as if to say "yes" can also add real positivity to your visualization. (Read more about affirmations on page 29.)

You can create a visualization for anything that you're trying to manifest. Just as it is important to repeat affirmations to make them work, revisit your visualizations regularly. The more you do it, the more you'll build up a positive mindset – and one that feels real and natural. As you radiate positivity, you'll send out vibrations to the universe that attract the good things back into your life, moving closer to manifesting your desires.

CREATE A VISION BOARD

. . . .

MANIFEST-OH! If you find the visualization process in the previous chapter tricky, focusing on something physical may work better for you. A terrific way to do this is to create a vision board. Clarity, inspiration and motivation – a vision board provides all the key elements to help you realise your dreams.

What's a vision board?

If you've redecorated you home, you may have made a mood board – a collage of colours, soft furnishings, furniture, etc., that helps you with ideas for creating the feel you want in a room. A vision board is similar, except that it visually represents something you want to manifest in your life. It uses the power of intention to generate those all-important good vibes needed to attract the universe's positive energy into your life.

WHAT YOU'LL NEED

A large piece of board, corkboard (if you're going to pin things) or thick card

Scissors and glue

Magazines, photos, quotes

Pens and markers

Alternatively, create a digital vision board.

What's your vision?

Identify what you want your vision board to focus on. For example, it could be finding love, getting your dream job or finding a forever home. Try to stick to one thing you want to manifest per board. Don't rush the process of creating your vision board – set aside time when you won't be interrupted. You don't have to finish it in one sitting. In fact, setting it aside for a day or so will give you time to reflect and new ideas may pop into your head.

Get started

- With your vision in mind, collect photos, pictures, quotes, affirmations and thoughts that represent your vision. They can be anything that conveys what it is you want to attract into your life. It's important that they give a sense of the positive emotions and feelings you associate with successfully manifesting your vision.

- Don't focus on just pictures. The board should represent how you want your future self to feel. You can do this by including descriptive words and quotes. Words such as 'strong' and 'confident' are good examples.

- Lay everything out on your board and make sure you're happy with the layout before you stick/pin anything into place. Use markers to write, draw arrows, circle specific items too – whatever works for you. Leave space so that you can add to your board. (Putting too much on your board can also distract from the focus.)

Remember, your vision board isn't set in stone. It should be able to change and grow, just as your journey towards manifesting your future will evolve.

How to use your vision board

Just as how you might stick positive affirmation post-its around your home, keep your vision board visible. Tidying it away in a cupboard is certainly not going to help manifest good things in your life. Keeping your board somewhere you'll see it every day (and often) reminds you of what you're working towards. It helps you maintain a clear vision. Feeling the positive emotions you've included on your board will encourage the good vibrations you need to successfully manifest your vision.

Sometimes you'll have challenging days when it feels like nothing is going right and you're moving further away from where you want to be in your life. Don't give up – spend time with your vision board. It will give you the visual pep talk you need to pick yourself up and keep following your dreams.

SOUND EFFECTS

. . . .

MANIFEST-OH! Sound is a wonderful thing when it comes to manifestation. With the right sounds you can calm your mind and change your vibrational energy, beaming your intentions into the universe even more powerfully.

Why sound?

For centuries, all around the world, sound has been used as a healing tool to restore physical and mental wellbeing. Just think how your favourite song or a tune with a particular beat can make you reflect on something – or in the opposite way, raise your spirits and fill you with energy and joy. Now you know why dancing around the kitchen is so wonderful for self-care!

As with so many things that lift our energy, we often take sound and music for granted. We don't really think about why they make us feel good, we just know they do. The secret ingredient is vibration (remember, the entire world is vibrating thanks to energy). All sounds have a frequency that affect your own internal vibrations – it follows that different frequencies can change your vibrations in different ways.

For example, a particular frequency might awaken your intuition or make you feel loved (or even encourage sexual arousal). Or think about a sudden, unexpected sound that shocks you, making your heart pound. Or the soundtrack to a horror film or thriller that has you on the edge of your seat. Sound can both promote and disrupt our harmony.

Sound and manifestation

We know that sound can make us vibrate in different ways, but how does that help us manifest our future? Sound is most definitely your manifestation friend. By using sound, you can amplify the vibrations of your own intentions, boosting the manifestation process. It's like hooking yourself up to a massive amp and pumping your positive energy and intentions into the universe with gusto. What's more, certain frequencies are better suited to helping you manifest in different areas. (They can even work with your chakras.)

When you're using sound, it's important to find what works for you. For example, if you find a particular instrument grating and it prevents you from getting into the 'zone', find something else. It's worth taking the time to experiment with different sounds and recordings so that you get the most out of the process.

The Solfeggio Frequencies

Dig into sound and manifestation more deeply and you'll discover the Solfeggio Frequencies. These are a series of six electromagnetic tones that Gregorian Monks used for meditative chanting. The frequencies deeply penetrate the conscious and subconscious mind and stimulate inner healing:

- **396 Hertz (Hz):** frees you from feelings of guilt and fear.
  Chakra – root.

- **417 Hz:** facilitates change in your life; relieves the conscious and subconscious mind from traumatic past experiences.
  Chakra – sacral.

- **528 Hz:** linked to transformation and miracles.
  Chakra – solar plexus.

- **639 Hz:** improves your connections and relationships with other
  people. Chakra – heart.

- **741 Hz:** linked to expressing yourself, helps you open up.
  Chakra – throat.

- **852 Hz:** develops your awareness and connects you to your intuition
  and spiritual self.
  Chakra – third eye.

Each chakra has its own frequency that it resonates with. Listening to
that frequency can help unlock any blockages in the chakra and release
your energy flow (see page 37).

Take a sound bath

This may sound like a holistic experience at the Glastonbury Festival,
but a sound bath is a perfectly simple practice that can be enjoyed in the
comfort of your own home. It is particularly good if you find standard
meditation practices difficult. Its purpose is to create a feeling of harmony,
removing discord from your energy field and clearing any blockages. The
combination of relaxation, clarity of thought and inner awareness will
amplify your positive vibrations as you send them into the universe, as
well as motivate you to manifest your goals.

Follow these simple steps:

- Set your intentions. How do you want to change your vibrational
  energy? What intention do you want to manifest? Choose a frequency

that connects to this. (You can find free sound recordings at different frequencies on the internet. See the Solfeggio Frequencies on page 44.)

- Find somewhere comfortable to sit or lie down. For the best results, listen to the sound through headphones to truly immerse yourself. Closing your eyes will also help you focus.

- As you tune into the sound, what are your thoughts? How does it make you feel? Think about your intentions and what it is you want to manifest in your life. Just go with the flow as much as possible and let yourself be swept along by the sounds. If your mind wanders, take a few slow breaths and then return your focus to your intention.

- Enjoy your sound bath for however long feels good to you. When starting out, try just a few minutes and build up the time the more you get into it.

Tools of the trade

You may find that a sound bath is enough for you. However, you can also introduce instruments and tools to your practice to aid meditation and relaxation. Many of these are from the percussion family and are designed to be tapped with a baton or your hands. Some play a single note and some play multiple notes, whilst others are unpitched. Below are some examples of instruments commonly used (all are easy to purchase for yourself):

- **Singing bowls:** Singing bowls have been used for centuries for meditation and healing. Research suggests sound meditation using the long, resonant tone of singing bowls helps to alleviate tension, anger, fatigue and low moods. You can add water to the bowl to create water sounds and make water particles dance to the frequency of the vibrations. The bowl can either be struck or stroked with a mallet to create a constant tone. It's not easy but it'll make you focus.

- **Tuning forks:** When not being used to tune an orchestra, tuning forks can be applied to various parts of the body to transfer vibrations through the skin to specific pressure points. They produce a long, consistent pitch, which makes them ideal for meditation.

- **Gongs:** The dynamic range of frequencies that a gong can produce is huge – from low, gentle sounds to mighty crashes that make you vibrate from the tips of your toes to the top of your head. Gongs are commonly used for sound baths and are great for balancing your chakras. (You may be able to find local groups where you can experience gong meditation.)

- **Tingsha cymbals:** These consist of two small metal cymbals joined with a cord. Tapped together they make a pure bell tone. Use them when you want to reach a calm, meditative state and achieve clarity of mind. They can also be rung to fix a moment in your memory; for example, when you are feeling full of positivity about the desires you want to manifest, ring the cymbals. Next time you ring them, you'll associate the sound with how you felt the previous time, recreating the positivity.

Simply hanging a wind chime in your garden or on your balcony can have positive effects too.

Good vibrations

Adding sound to your manifestation toolbox can help you achieve your goals. It can encourage your internal vibrations to send positivity into the universe and increase the likelihood of attracting positive change into your life. As with all the techniques in the book, experiment a little and you'll learn a lot about yourself and what you're capable of.

SAY THANK YOU

. . . .

MANIFEST-OH! Gratitude – feeling thankful – lets us see the fullness of life. It helps us step back and get some perspective, especially when it feels like life isn't going our way. Gratitude can bring a sense of calm and balance. And, of course, it's all about those all-important vibrations.

What is gratitude?

Gratitude is not about being a Pollyanna, that is, being excessively positive or optimistic about everything. As real people living a very real life, we know that sometimes life is going to be difficult. You might be a mystic channelling the power of the universe, but life can still be sh*t.

What gratitude does is teach us how to count our blessings and to say 'thank you' for the good things in our life. When we do that, we usually see that the positives outweigh the negatives. Our sense of perspective is restored.

We can also feel gratitude when bad things happen. For example, you break up with a long-term partner and your heart feels like it's breaking. Stop and say to yourself: "Yes, this is tough but are there things I can feel grateful for?" You might feel thankful for having some 'me-time' back or perhaps you've always said 'no' to a holiday with friends because you felt it should be time spent with your partner. And, boy, do you love having the bed back to yourself. Gratitude makes us appreciate that things aren't so bad after all. Look for good in your situation.

"Gratitude is the healthiest of all human emotions. The more you express gratitude for what you have, the more likely you will have even more to express gratitude for."

Pablo Picasso

Gratitude and manifestation

The positive energy that comes with gratitude makes you vibrate at a higher frequency. Along with joy, freedom and love, gratitude is one of the highest frequencies you can emit – and it's a frequency the universe responds to with abundance. It's the law of attraction at work again.

When you feel gratitude, the universe gives you more things to appreciate. You then feel even more thankful and a wonderful circle of gratitude emerges. Life feels good and your desires start to manifest themselves thick and fast. When your gratitude is running high, you're effectively opening your arms wide to the universe and saying, "Thank you, I'm ready for more good stuff – send it my way!"

It's important to know that gratitude can't be faked. You can't trick the universe into manifesting your future. For your vibrational energy to work, you need to feel your gratitude, not just go through the motions of saying the right words. (The same applies to positive affirmations and visualisation – you must feel them to believe them and to make them work effectively.)

Let's find out how to make gratitude part of your everyday life …

Keep a gratitude journal

A gratitude journal is a fantastic way to acknowledge the positive things in life and get your vibrational frequency buzzing. Set aside time each day to write down what made you feel happy and thankful that day. Even if you only spend five minutes writing, you'll soon start to see improvements in your mindset:

- An increase in positive thinking – combatting negative feelings and worry.
- Greater compassion and empathy for others.
- Increased resilience to the challenges life throws at you.

If you're struggling to think what to write (it does take a little practice, especially if you're used to negative feelings or are self-critical), try one of these prompts:

- Who or what inspired you today?
- What happened today that showed you're on the way to manifesting your future?
- An act of kindness someone showed you.
- What can you see from your window that you're grateful for?
- Something unexpected that happened (obviously not something that made you jump out of your skin!).
- A gift or a compliment you received.
- Something that made you feel proud.
- Did the universe send something good your way today?

Some days you'll find it harder to know what to write. In those instances, it's okay just to write down one thing. Every positive counts, so focus on that one thing and use it to boost your vibrational energy.

Sleep on it

Not everyone is lucky enough to fall straight to sleep when their head hits the pillow. It might be the time you find yourself worrying the most or have endless negative thoughts running through your head. "What if I don't get the promotion I want?" "What if I fail?" ('What ifs' are a terrible thing.)

When you go to bed, think of three things you're grateful for. List them in your head or write them on a piece of paper and pop it under your pillow. Focus on the three things and how they make you feel. Tuning into that positive frequency will help you to relax, but it will also ensure that the last thing you do before you go to sleep is transmit good vibrations to the universe. Those vibrations will continue through the night, rewiring your subconscious thought patterns to change the way you talk to yourself and your automatic reactions to situations. In the morning, remind yourself of the three things you were grateful for so that you carry that positivity with you into the day.

So, let the law of attraction work whilst you sleep. It's a simple technique that can make a significant difference. Try it.

Gratitude affirmations

Everything you've already learnt about affirmations (see page 29) can be applied to gratitude. Remember, repetition is key, as is feeling and believing the words – not simply saying them. You can write gratitude affirmations of your own that align with what you're trying to manifest. Below are some ideas to get you started:

- I am grateful for all the dreams I am manifesting.

- I am grateful that the universe is listening to me.
- I am grateful for every improvement I see, however small.
- I am grateful that I am learning and growing.
- I am grateful that things keep getting better and better.
- I am grateful for the love and support of the people around me.
- I am grateful that I have resources within myself to manifest my dreams.
- I am grateful for the power to create change.

Your affirmations can be general or specific, but they must make you feel emotion to create the right vibrations. It can be empowering if the affirmations reflect a sense of moving forwards on a journey towards manifesting the life you want.

Thank you

Expressing gratitude is a mindset that requires practice, particularly if you're not used to it. When you're not repeating your affirmations or writing in your gratitude journal, always remember to say 'thank you'. It could be to another person when they hold a door for you, or it could be to the universe when unexpected money arrives at a time when you most need it. Get into the habit of saying 'thank you' – and appreciating why you're saying thank you and how you feel – and you'll start to carry a permanent positive force field with you everywhere you go.

CONNECT TO THE EARTH

. . . .

MANIFEST–OH! Our modern lifestyles have taken us further and further away from the ground we walk on. Reconnecting with the earth to balance our mind and body is essential to creating the right mindset to manifest your desires.

Why is the earth so special?

Did you know that the surface of the earth carries an electrical charge that vibrates at different frequencies? The earth's electrons have a subtle negative charge that helps keep the rest of the world in balance – including you. Unfortunately, as humans, we've become less and less connected to the earth. Our shoes have synthetic soles that don't conduct electricity, our beds are lifted off the ground, we live in high-rise apartments … the list goes on.

Earthing

Earthing – also known as grounding – restores your connection to the earth. This allows the earth to transfer its electrical energy to you, balancing your own energy flow. Our whole body works through electrical transmissions – our brain, thoughts, muscles – and if these are out of synch, our bodies don't function as well as they could. The more we connect with the earth, the more our internal energy is stabilised and attains its natural state. The benefits of grounding for your physical and emotional wellbeing are wide-ranging. Research suggests that reconnecting with the earth might, amongst other benefits: promote better sleep, reduce muscle pain and inflammation, lower stress levels, reduce fatigue, improve blood flow and aid digestion. The good news is that earthing is simple and nothing but pleasurable.

How does it help you manifest?

Connecting to the earth grounds you in the present, firmly in the here and now. Without that grounding we are unstable and prone to getting distracted and losing our way. This isn't helpful if you're trying to move forward on your manifestation journey. On that journey, you need clarity of mind and focus, both of which are necessary to keep your intentions on track. If you can't see and feel your path, you are highly likely to stray from it.

A little note on chakras

Earthing puts your roots back into the ground, providing nourishment, stability and growth. This is very much the function of your root chakra (see page 26). Earthing is an effective way to support and unblock this chakra. When your energy is flowing through your root chakra, you'll also find it easier to draw up energy from the earth.

"*Feel yourself grounded to the earth, while your mind is focusing on the sky of clarity.*"

Nawang Khechog

Top tips for earthing

You can earth yourself indoors but this often involves 'devices' you need to purchase. So, in the interests of inclusivity, we're only looking here at earthing outdoors!

Go barefoot walking or running

(Being in your socks works too.) This is best done on grass, sand or dirt. Start off with around half an hour a day. Feel the warmth and the moisture on the soles of your feet and visualize the earth's energy flowing upwards into your body. (Obviously watch out you don't step on anything sharp, dog poo or creatures that sting!)

Lay on the ground

Feel the sensation of the earth beneath you and press your hands into the ground. Watch the clouds float by. As you breathe out, imagine yourself melting into the earth.

Take your work outside

As people continue to work from home after the COVID pandemic, this is a convenient option for many. However, if you are in an office, use your lunch hour to get outside and sit on a grassy area.

Wild or open water swimming

Swimming in the sea, a lake or river is a great way to ground yourself. Enjoy the sensation of the cool water and the stones, sand and rocks under your feet. But make sure you do this safely – online research will help you discover the best places to swim.

Gardening

Gardening is an amazing way to get your hands dirty and delve into a connection with the earth. Even if you're simply weeding or dead heading flowers, it is an absorbing pastime that focuses you in the now. It's no wonder that gardening is starting to be prescribed by doctors for anxiety and depression. Caring for plants is about growth, mirroring the tending and nourishing needed for your own personal growth as you work towards manifesting your future.

Earthing is specifically about connecting with the energy on the surface of the earth. Being in nature more generally is also uplifting for your spirit and harnesses the energies of the universe. The next chapter takes you on that wonderful journey into nature.

HARNESS NATURE

. . . .

MANIFEST-OH! Getting back to nature has long been a way of escaping the rat race. But it's not just about ticking boxes (wi-fi off, phone off, walking boots on – check!) and then re-joining the throng. If you embrace nature in your life, it can give you a whole new perspective and set you on the path to successful manifestation. Nature is a powerful force.

The Great Outdoors

Getting outside has an amazing ability to replenish your energy stores, especially if it takes you away from something that's draining you. Perhaps you're struggling with a challenging work task or your kids' demands are driving you insane, or maybe you're worrying about the future. When you feel drained, it's easy to become overwhelmed and lose your sense of perspective.

When you're manifesting, losing your perspective is troublesome. It's not just a wobble on your bike – it's falling off! You might lose your trust in the process and your belief in yourself. Spending time in nature is one way to renew your perspective and clarity of mind. It provides that feeling of being part of something bigger – the universe – where everything is connected and working together. Just as you need it to.

Plus, one of the wonderful things about nature is that it's free!

Enjoy the elements

The perfect way to embrace nature is to surrender to it. To use a corny phrase, "be at one with the universe"! Here are some suggestions for how to immerse yourself:

- Rain brings nature to life – the smells, the colours, the squelch of mud, the splash of puddles. Get your waterproofs on (or just brave it) and get out there and enjoy yourself. You could even get naked in your garden in the rain and embrace your inner child.

- If wild or sea swimming doesn't appeal, go swimming in an outdoor pool as the rain falls.

- Visit the coast and listen to waves rolling and crashing. This can be meditative, allowing you to tune in, focus and relax.

- Close your eyes and listen to nature – leaves moving in the wind, birds, insects. You don't even need to be outside – just open a window wide.

- Check back to Connect to the Earth (page 53) for more ideas.

"We depend on nature not only for our physical survival, we also need nature to show us the way home, the way out of the prison of our own minds."

Eckhart Tolle

Forest bathing

Unwind and connect with nature with *shinrin-yoku* – 'forest bathing'. Originating in Japan, this is the practice of immersing yourself in nature and fully engaging your five senses to relax and experience everything around you.

It's about spending quiet, mindful time to improve your wellbeing. You don't need to find a huge forest to do this. Any woodland will do, but it does help to feel as if you're away from it all, enveloped by trees. And turn off your phone!

- Focus on your breath and on breathing in the fresh air around you. As you breathe more deeply, your body will start to relax.

- Don't rush; it's not a race to get around the forest as quickly as you can. Stay for as long as possible. The slower you go, the more you'll notice around you.

- Use your senses. What can you see, smell, hear and touch? How does it make you feel?

Forest bathing will leave you feeling calm and rejuvenated. A good couple of hours will work wonders, but you'll be surprised how little time is needed to feel the effects.

Nature and manifestation

When you're outdoors, think about the whole ecosystem. How the sun and rain nourish the earth that the plants and trees emerge from; how the wildlife relies on the forest for food and life; how the bees pollinate the flowers. Remind yourself that you, too, are part of this amazing system. When it's balanced and working in harmony, it flourishes. This is exactly what you are aiming for with the techniques in this book: to create an inner calm and strength that works beautifully in harmony with the universe. Only then will you reap the rewards of the law of attraction and manifest your future.

WORK WITH THE PLANET

· · · · · · · · · · · · · · · · · · · ·

MANIFEST-OH! To be in harmony with the universe, you need to be mindful of working with it, not against it. This means being environmentally conscious and living sustainably. If you want the universe to be kind to you and help you manifest your future, you need to show your gratitude by being equally kind in return.

Your planet needs you

Planet Earth sustains us. Unfortunately, humans have done so much damage to the planet that it is now struggling to support us in the same way. Human history has been a lot about taking from the planet – without giving back to balance this out and restore harmony. We can't reverse the damage we've done; however, we can make our own individual contributions to slow down any further destruction.

The chapter on gratitude (see page 48) talks about the reciprocal relationship between yourself and the universe. By looking after the planet and doing your bit to restore the equilibrium, you are saying 'thank you' to the universe. Thanks to the law of attraction, the more you give and give thanks for, the more the universe will reward you by manifesting your desires.

What can you do?

As a modern mystic, you're conscious of the environment, your impact on it and how to live sustainably. However, if you've not 'gone green' yet and aren't sure how to, here are some tips to get started. If you're already the greenest of mystics, there may be some new ideas to build on the great work you're doing.

Plastic

- Stop using single-use plastics (e.g. straws, water bottles). Stick to reusable and refillable items.

- Take your own bags with you when you go shopping.

- Ditch packaging by buying your fruit and veg loose.

- Find out it there's a 'refill' shop close by – simply take along reusable containers and fill them with the goods you need.

- Choose products packaged in boxes – cardboard is far easier to recycle than plastic.

- Rather than a disposable razor, use a razor with replaceable blades.

In the kitchen

- Aim for zero food waste – get creative with leftovers and use the bits you wouldn't normally think to use (the green tops of carrots make a lovely pesto!). If you can't use it, compost it.

- Buy local and reduce the number of miles food travels to your table.

- If you're a meat-eater, cut out one serving of meat per week. Meat is the most resource-intensive of foods.

- Use coffee grounds and tea leaves to give the plants in your garden an extra boost!

Be water conscious

- Fix leaks. It might seem like it's only a drip, but a tap dripping for months wastes a huge amount of water.

- Limit your showers to four minutes max. (Remember, too, that showers use less water than baths.)

- Only put your washing machine or dishwasher on when it's fully loaded. Use the economy setting.

- Turn off the tap when brushing your teeth.

- Save wastewater in the kitchen (e.g. from washing vegetables) to water your plants and garden. Ditch packaging by buying your fruit and veg loose.

- Use a watering can in the garden instead of a sprinkler or a hosepipe. (And collect rainwater in a water butt if you can.)

Save energy

- Don't leave appliances on standby.

- Turn your thermostat down by 1 degree.

- Newly bought appliances should have a good energy-efficiency rating.

- Turn lights off when you leave a room.

- Don't block heaters and radiators with large pieces of furniture.

- Dry laundry outside rather than using a tumble dryer.

- Make sure your home is well insulated.

Go the extra mile

- Get involved in local environmental projects – or start your own.

- Organise a litter pick.

- Walk, cycle or take public transport if you can.
- Recycle, reuse, repurpose, revamp, resell, reinvent!

And so, the magic starts to work ...

Trying to do the best you can for the planet has many rewards. You'll be doing your bit to restore harmony to the universe, renewing its positive energy. When you make a difference, you'll feel a sense of achievement and your confidence grows. This is the ideal mindset for manifestation.

MEDITATE TO MANIFEST

....

MANIFEST–OH! Meditation encourages the clarity of mind and self–insight needed to understand who you truly are. Only then can you discover what you really want in life and start to manifest those desires.

Meditation: the benefits

The benefits of mediation are widely acknowledged. It's practiced all over the world by those seeking to calm their minds and bodies in a world where stress is the norm. When practiced regularly, even just a few minutes of meditation can have positive effects.

But how does meditation help you with manifesting?

Find your true self

When you meditate you look inwards, cutting through all the noise to find your true self. You see through everything you think you should be doing and that society has conditioned you to believe are appropriate goals. What you thought you wanted in life becomes insignificant and you uncover new goals that reflect your true life purpose.

It's these intentions you can then work towards manifesting as you grow into your best self. The truer the intentions are to you, the more likely it is they will become reality.

New perspectives

Meditating gives you a sense of perspective on what does and doesn't matter in life. It helps you weed those things out of your life that aren't helpful and those thoughts that are harmful. You're left with the freedom to pursue your dreams unburdened.

Your inner voice

If you meditate regularly, you'll find it easier to recognize and hear your 'inner voice' – your intuition. It's the gut feeling that tells you that a certain path will be the right one to take on your journey towards manifesting your future. Manifestation requires you to trust in the universe, but you also need to trust your intuition. This is especially true when we find ourselves out of our comfort zone or having to take a risk (often in defiance of everything our rational brain is screaming at us!).

Open your mind

As mediation calms our mind, our mind becomes more receptive and open to new ideas. What you thought were obstacles to manifesting your future might suddenly melt away as you see more clearly the direction you need to take. You become more receptive to all the possibilities available to you and accept that you have the power within you to manifest them.

Improve your focus

How often do you make yourself sit still and concentrate? Probably not very often, especially in an age where something electronic always seems to be pinging us. Meditation restores our attention span and teaches us to tune out distractions. When you're setting your intentions and goals, you need to have this focus. To manifest your future, you must keep your goals in sight, avoiding unhelpful distractions along the way.

Exercise

If you've not tried meditation before, this exercise introduces you to the key techniques: focus, breath and stillness.

1. Sit or lie down comfortably. Close your eyes and breathe naturally.

2. Notice your breath and how your body moves as you breathe in and out. Focus on your breath without controlling its speed or how deeply you're breathing. Let your thoughts drift by and give them no attention. If your mind wanders, just move your focus back to your breath.

3. Continue for two to three minutes initially. As you get more practiced, meditation becomes easier and you can extend the time.

Just 10 minutes of meditation a day will have a positive impact. You should start to notice a difference within a few weeks.

Chakra meditation

You can use meditation to cleanse and realign your chakras. If your chakras are blocked, your energy doesn't flow freely around your body and your emotional and physical states are disturbed. Balanced chakras create harmony of mind, body and spirit – the perfect state for working with the universe to manifest your goals. (If you need to refresh your memory on chakras, head back to page 24.)

Chakra meditation can target one specific chakra. For example, a heart chakra meditation might focus on the colour green or on feelings of love and harmony. Alternatively, you can go for a complete overhaul and target all your chakras in one meditation session. This is useful if you're not sure where the blockages are. Also, given that your chakras work as a holistic whole, meditating on all of them will have the greatest benefit.

Exercise

Try this exercise to rebalance your entire system:

1. Sit on the floor in a comfortable position. Breathe deeply and evenly.

2. Visualize each chakra, starting from your root chakra and moving up to your crown. At each chakra point, imagine the energy flowing through that chakra. You can also visualize their colour.

3. Spend 3–4 minutes focusing on each chakra. Only move on to the next one when you can imagine and feel the energy flowing freely through the chakra you're visualizing.

4. If your mind wanders, simply take a breath and then refocus on your chakra. It takes practice to remain focused, so don't beat yourself up if you struggle at first.

5. When you've moved through all your chakras, slowly bring you awareness back to the room. Gently wiggle your fingers and toes and have a lovely stretch.

When you have a good understanding of how your chakras work and can identify which chakra is blocked from how you're feeling, you can try meditating on an individual chakra.

There's so much to discover on this topic – far more than the space in this book allows. Take time to explore, for example, different meditation positions and mudras (hand gestures that help the flow of energy). You can find some excellent resources on the internet.

Meditation using affirmations

Whilst you're meditating, your mind becomes more receptive to new thoughts and ideas. It's therefore an ideal time to focus on your affirmations. (See the chapter on affirmations on page 29.) If we're not used to talking positively to ourselves, affirmations can be hard to accept. When we say affirmations with a relaxed, open mind, they meet less resistance and are more likely to settle in our subconscious and change our thought patterns.

Manifestation requires us to believe in our intentions to work, so meditating using affirmations is a valuable technique for your toolbox.

Exercise

1. Sit in a comfortable position. Close your eyes and take five deep breaths (in through your nose, out through your mouth). Then breathe normally.

2. When you feel relaxed, think about your first affirmation (for example, "I am on the path to achieving my goals"). Repeat the affirmation either aloud or silently to yourself.

3. As you repeat the affirmation, feel what it means to you and visualize how it looks. For example, if your affirmation is "I am going to get the job", how does it feel to have got the job and be doing it? What are you wearing on the first day as you stride confidently through the doors?

4. You can take a break from repeating your affirmations and simply continue to focus on your breath. Return to your affirmations when you're ready.

5. Slowly bring your awareness back to the room and open your eyes. The strong warmth you felt from your affirmations will continue beyond the end of your meditation practice – enjoy!

Start off by practising for 10 minutes and gradually build up the time as you become comfortable with the process. As with affirmations more generally, the more regularly you meditate using them, the sooner they'll settle in your mind and become second nature. And, of course, the sooner you'll see your intentions manifest in your life.

BE MINDFUL

. . . .

MANIFEST-OH! Mindfulness is about the present moment. You might ask how that helps with manifestation, which is about shaping your future reality? It's all about having a positive mindset and no distractions.

What is mindfulness?

Mindfulness is a technique that focuses on the present. What can we see? What can we hear? Like connecting to nature (see pages 53 and 58), it opens our senses and lets us appreciate what is going on around us in the moment. It helps us step back from 'living in our heads' where we're thinking about the past or worrying about the future but letting the here and now pass us by. It releases us from those negative thoughts that hold us back from believing in our dreams.

The benefits of mindful living

- Reduces stress and worry.

- Strengthens your mental resilience and ability to handle life's challenges.

- Reduces harmful and negative emotions, for example anger and fear.

- Improves your focus.

- Increases your sense of happiness and fulfilment.

Embracing mindfulness

The hardest thing about making mindfulness part of your life is remembering to do it. Luckily, it can be practiced anywhere and without anyone noticing. So, grab any moments in your day when you have spare time. It doesn't have to be when you're feeling stressed, it can be whilst you're waiting for an appointment or on your commute. Plus, it's a better use of time than swiping through TikTok on your phone. You can bring mindfulness into your life by taking up activities like yoga (see page 78), tai-chi and meditation (see page 66), all of which focus on breathing and relaxation. You can also use simple mindfulness techniques to reap the benefits in a very short time – more on that to follow. How can you include mindfulness in manifesting your future?

- Mindfulness helps you relate to your thoughts and emotions in a new way. Like with meditation, it gives you greater clarity of mind. By clearing away all the 'noise' in your head, you improve your awareness of who you are and what you want in life. These are the foundations for setting the intentions you want to manifest.

- Mindfulness enhances your appreciation of the world, creating a more positive mindset and the higher vibrations that set the law of attraction in motion.

- When you're not sure manifestation is working, you may feel disheartened or overwhelmed. Mindfulness is perfect for moments when you need to reduce your stress levels so you can see the bigger picture. It clears your mind of worrying about the future (and the past), knocking those nasty 'what ifs' on the head and allowing you to reset and regroup.

- Mindfulness is great for preparing you for many of the techniques discussed in this book. Whether it be setting your goals and intentions, visualization or running your spiritual bath, all these benefit from the focus, self-awareness and serenity that mindfulness provides.

How to have a mindful moment

Mindfulness can be practiced anywhere and without anyone noticing. Even a few minutes of practice can put you back on track if you're having a wobble. Try this exercise.

1. Stop what you're doing and bring your awareness to everything around you. Breathe deeply and evenly. What can you see? Look at things in more detail than you normally would. Pick out the tiny things that would ordinarily pass you by. What can you hear and smell? Move your fingers – what textures can you feel?

2. Consider what thoughts are going through your head. Let them pass by without dwelling on them (especially any negative thoughts), as if you're watching clouds float by. (As all mystics know, troubles are merely clouds passing by before the sun appears again.)

3. Scan your body with your mind. Are you tensing any muscles? If you are, relax them.

4. Continue with the above, breathing evenly and feeling a sense of calm enveloping you.

5. When you're ready to bring your mindful moment to a close, take a few seconds to feel gratitude for the wonder of the universe around you and the calmness and energy you draw from it.

GIVE SOMETHING BACK

. . . .

MANIFEST–OH! Modern mystics have a strong sense of justice. You strive to find ways to improve the world around you and to make a better future not just for yourself but for others. You know that the actions you take now shape the future.

Can you make the world a better place?

To make the world a better place sounds like a tall order. However, if it is your passion and you can break it down into smaller goals, there's no reason it shouldn't be one of your intentions. Individual actions might not always change the world but they do make a difference. When you combine lots of people making a small contribution, the impact can be huge. You are not powerless – you're very much the opposite. By using manifestation and taking practical steps, you have the power to change lives.

So, how can you do your bit to create a better world using everything you know about manifestation and the law of attraction? (See also Work with the Planet on page 62.)

What impact do you want to have?

When you set your intentions, think about where your passions lie. Do you want to contribute to a social issue, such as the mental health of young people? Or is animal welfare something you feel strongly about? Your intentions could be:

- I want young people to have somewhere to go when they need emotional support.

- I want to run a business that supports people with disabilities.

- I want all children in my local community to have access to a breakfast.

- I want to create a successful campaign to raise awareness of young onset dementia.

Is it something you'd need to start from scratch? (Some people affected by an issue set up a charity, for example.) Or is work already happening in this area where you could volunteer your time and expertise? Also consider the scope of the change you want to make – it could be at a local level; it doesn't have to be global.

Practical steps

Manifestation doesn't happen by waiting for the universe to deliver what you want. You need to put the work in. That means taking practical action:

- **Volunteer:** Charities and organisations are always on the lookout for committed volunteers. You can either contact them directly or approach an organization that co-ordinates volunteers for charities and community groups. To make a difference, you can do something as simple as hand out leaflets or help out at an event. It may be that you have expertise in a particular area that could be of assistance. What is important is being there and taking part.

- **Raise money:** There are endless ways to raise money for worthy causes – cake sales, marathons and, of course, the obligatory skydive, to name just a few!

- **Start your own campaign:** There is nothing to stop you grasping the bull by the horns if someone hasn't already!

Spread good vibrations

Volunteering and campaigning have lots of positive benefits. Your confidence and self-esteem will bloom and you'll learn new skills. When you're exposed to other people's experiences, you also re-evaluate your own priorities in life and discover what's important to you. We know that manifestation only works if you really want something. When you feel good about what you're doing and can see a positive impact, your energy will vibrate at a higher frequency. This attracts positive things into your life.

But it's not just about YOU. Your good vibrations are also working to create positive outcomes for those people around you. These are the people working to change the world like you are, along with those who benefit from it. Your positivity will radiate from you and touch everyone it encounters, empowering them to pursue their own dreams of manifesting a better future. The more people there are with a strong life purpose that aligns with their true self, the more harmony there is in the universe. Giving something back – and showing love and compassion (something yoga teaches, see page 80) – can be truly life changing.

PRACTICE YOGA

. . . .

*MANIFEST-OH! Whether you're someone who has never
laid a foot on a yoga mat, a beginner or a seasoned pro,
you might not have considered the part yoga can play in
manifesting your future. As a transformational spiritual
practice that balances mind, body and spirit, it provides
the self-awareness and calm you need to be in
harmony with the universe.*

Why yoga?

Yoga is great for your strength and flexibility, but it is also incredible for
your mind and spirit. It draws on the power of postures, movement and
breath to create clarity and focus and promote inner stillness.

If you're new to yoga, don't be put off by all the yogis doing headstands
and handstands on social media. Yoga is for everyone, whatever your
shape, ability or fitness level. If you're an experienced yogi already (and
one of those people upside down on Instagram), you'll understand that
yoga is an ongoing physical and spiritual journey. In fact, very much like
the journey you take when you choose to manifest your future.

Yoga and manifestation

With so many other tools and techniques to choose from, why should
you make yoga part of your manifestation? Yoga is the perfect way to

tune our minds to a higher frequency and calm ourselves down. It lets you experience a feeling of connectedness – to other people and to the universe.

Rediscover your inner self

To understand what you want to manifest, it is vital to understand 'you'. This is your inner self – your essence. It's the 'you' that is separate from the job you do, where you live, your worries and external influences. In the modern world, we can become disconnected from our inner self. Yoga helps you rediscover that inner core and empowers it. Only by understanding who we are, what we want and why we want it can we successfully create the future we desire.

Gratitude

Yoga teaches us to be grateful. It teaches us to be thankful for what we have, rather than focus on what we lack. Gratitude is a powerful emotion that fills you with positive energy and good vibrations. It creates one of the highest frequencies you can emit and one which the universe readily responds to (see Say Thank You, page 48).

When you are grateful for what you have every step of the way, the future you're working towards is more likely to manifest.

Balance your chakras

Yoga postures move your energy through your body and balance your chakras (see page 28). When your energy is flowing freely through your body, you feel greater spiritual harmony and physical and emotional wellbeing.

Compassion

Yoga teaches us about compassion, both to ourselves and to others. The law of attraction sends that love right back to us and allows our manifestations to become reality.

Unity

Yoga teaches unity, that there is no separation between 'the doer, the act of doing and that which is done'. This extends to manifestation. You are already part of the future you want to create – it is inside you, it is your

life purpose. Practicing yoga and meditation will help you understand, as well as find what is within you. Yoga will empower you to turn those dreams into reality.

> *"The success of Yoga does not lie in the ability to perform postures but in how it positively changes the way we live our life and our relationships."*
>
> T. K. V. Desikachar

Have a go

If you're not already doing yoga, it's easy to find classes in your area. Try a few different ones – there are distinctive styles of yoga and teachers all have their own approach. You may find that some suit you better than others. It needs to feel 'right' for you – and if you aren't ready to try yoga as part of a group, there are also plenty of online videos.

There are a number of poses that are believed to be helpful when trying to manifest your intentions. The list below is by no means exhaustive. (Don't force yourself into any positions that your body isn't comfortable with yet and remember to breathe!). Here are five yoga poses for manifestation:

1. Sukhasana
The perfect pose in which to
contemplate what you'd like to
manifest and why.

2. Cobra
A powerful backbend that opens
your heart to all emotions and
lets you embrace the possibility
of positive change – the ideal
energy for manifestation.

3. Reverse Warrior
All warrior poses are about
channelling inner strength at the
same time as having gentleness
and balance in your life.

4. Boat

This isn't an easy one on the abs but it's well worth persevering with. A strong core gives you confidence in your aspirations. Don't forget to open your heart space in this pose.

5. Locust

This pose ensures spine is strong, keeping you driven and powerful – the qualities you need to overcome obstacles and remain focused on your manifestation.

A NOTE – KUNDALINI YOGA

Kundalini yoga helps you channel powerful energy thought to be 'coiled' at the base of your spine. When that energy is uncoiled, you reach a higher state of consciousness. It is a powerful form of yoga and is thought to be the style that aligns best with manifesting. However, because of the impact kundalini yoga can have, it is recommended that you only practice it with a trained practitioner.

OTHER TOOLS TO TRY

. . . .

MANIFEST-OH! This book is only a short guide for the modern mystic – and there's so much more to tell you. Some you'll learn for yourself as you become experienced at manifesting and continue your journey of self-discovery. There are lots of 'tried and tested' methods to manifest your future and some of these are included below. Remember, the important thing is to find what works for you. Not everything will, but don't be disheartened – when you find what is right for you, you'll know.

A letter from your future self

Write yourself a letter from the future in which you've manifested your intentions. Tell your current self about what you've achieved, how it feels and the difference it has made to your life. Be imaginative and use positive and emotive language. Imagining you are that person and embracing what it feels like will make this a powerful visualization exercise. This is a great one to do if you're feeling any wobbles and want to get back on track.

The 55 x 5 method

If you're researching manifestation, you'll notice that the 55 x 5 method is frequently mentioned. It is done over 5 days so make sure what you're trying to manifest is realistic in that timescale. For example, it's good if you want to deliver a fantastic speech the following week, but not so helpful if you want to become a millionaire by Friday! Choose what it is you want to manifest. Be specific and keep it small-scale. Write down your manifestation 55 times. It's important to stay focused as you write so do it at a time when you're not going to be distracted or interrupted. As you write, imagine how it feels to have achieved your intention. Repeat this every day for five days. Then let the universe do its work!

The 3-6-9 method

Another number method. This is based on the belief that the numbers 3, 6 and 9 have spiritual significance. Some believe that the number 3 represents 'energy', the number 6 is 'frequency' and number 9 is 'vibration'. When you combine the numbers, you therefore have the perfect foundation for manifestation. Create your intention in the form of an affirmation in the future tense (see page 30). For example, "I am grateful to be working with animals". When you wake up in the morning, write your affirmation down three times. In the middle of your day, write it down six times. Then, before you go to bed, write it down nine times. Do this for 33 days in a row.

Be patient

Remember to be patient and trust the universe – the manifestation may work within the 33 days or it may take a little longer.

keep
on
track

Whilst you are manifesting, it is helpful to know whether things are going in the right direction. As much as you must trust in the universe, it's only human to want to see results. The next section provides guidance and tips to help keep your manifestation journey smooth and fruitful.

TEN SIGNS FROM THE UNIVERSE

. . . .

MANIFEST-OH! How can you tell if manifestation and the law of attraction are working? What should you be aware of? Don't spend too much time looking for indications that your hard work is paying off. You need to trust that the universe is fulfilling its half of the bargain!

The signs to look out for

1. You are feeling optimistic and no longer worried about not achieving what you want in the future.

2. You start seeing angel numbers. These are numbers that keep occurring in your everyday life, which seem like a coincidence but have a meaning.

3. Synchronicity – two things happen that initially seem coincidental. For example, you want to manifest a job at a particular company and the next day you get one of their marketing leaflets through your door. Or perhaps you start hearing your favourite song playing in unusual places.

4. You see signs of your intentions everywhere. These could be people, symbols or objects relating to what you want to manifest.

5. You have a clear idea of the next steps you need to take. Trust in your intuition – it's pushing you to take that next step.

6. Random opportunities start arising. They might not always be obvious and you might dismiss them initially. Keep an open mind as they could be a sign from the universe.

7. You meet people who could play a part in your manifestation process. For example, you accept a last-minute invitation to a dinner party and find yourself sitting next to someone who works for your dream company.

8. The universe sends you a test to see how serious you are about your goals. You might find that an obstacle appears that could potentially knock you off track. Are you resilient enough to overcome it and stay firmly focused on what you want to manifest?

9. Things feel like they're happening at the right place at the right time. For example, you get an unexpected tax refund at the very moment you're about to cancel a holiday because you're struggling to afford it.

10. You have dreams about your manifestations. (Dreams also give an insight into your subconscious and the reasons why you're doing what you're doing.)

> *"If you can dream it,*
> *you can do it."*
>
> *Walt Disney*

HELP! IT'S NOT WORKING!

....

MANIFEST–OH! ... or it can a more deflated "OH". The journey to manifesting your intentions won't always be a smooth one or take the route you expected. If you're new to manifestation, this can leave you feeling downhearted. But don't panic.

Why isn't it working?

Let's change that to "why doesn't it feel like it's working?". If you've been doing the right things with the right mindset, it is highly likely that things are starting to happen. You may not have recognized they are or they're simply manifesting slowly. Manifesting requires practice. You're not doing anything wrong, but it could be that a few tweaks are needed. That's all part of the wonderful process through which we learn and grow.

Your manifestation health check

- **Take stock.** Set aside quiet time to think about your intentions. Do they still set your heart alight? If not, you may need to adjust them. It's not unusual for your intentions to change slightly – remember, life isn't a linear journey. To start seeing results, tweak your intentions so that they realign with what you want and lift your heart again. This will keep you travelling in the right direction.

- **Reboot your energy.** Is your energy working for you? Are the vibrations you're sending to the universe strong and positive? If you're worrying about something – perhaps you're fearful of failure – your energy is affected. Is someone pulling your vibrational energy down with unhelpful comments or behaviour? Think about what might be holding you back and work on that. (See What's Stopping You? on page 13.)

- **Action.** Remember, manifestation isn't magic! Your dreams won't just fall into your lap because you've put a crystal in the corner of a room. You need to put the work in. Think about whether the practical steps you're taking and your mindset are complementing the manifestation process.

- **Believe, believe, believe!** If you're only *thinking* about your goals, rather than *feeling* and *believing* them, you will struggle to manifest them. Belief in your intentions (and self-belief in your ability to achieve them) is the driving force behind manifestation.

- **Go with the flow.** Are you focused on manifestation happening in a particular way, at a particular time? Be prepared for manifestation happening in its own way. If you're not flexible, you could well miss things because you're not looking in the right direction. Trust in the universe to fulfil its part of the bargain too.

- **Are you sure it's not working?** Are you really, really, REALLY sure? Open your mind and look around you. Have you missed those tiny signs that manifestation is working? They won't all be obvious.

Running through the points above will set you back on the right track. Manifestation isn't easy – you'll make mistakes and that's okay. But, importantly, don't give up.

DOS AND DON'TS

· ·

You've made it to the end of the book! Here are some dos and don'ts to keep you on the path to successfully manifesting your future. You'll learn plenty of tips for yourself along the way – that's all part of the journey. Trust in what you learn, what the universe teaches you and, of course, your own intuition.

DO

- Go with the flow.

- Be patient – when the timing is right, things will happen.

- Trust that the universe will deliver.

- Be specific and consistent about what you want to manifest and attract into your life.

- Make manifestation part of your life – practice it every day.

- Meditate, visualize, repeat your affirmations. This will balance your energy flow and keep your mind clear, relaxed and focused on the power within you.

- Feel gratitude and appreciation for what you have and for the changes that are coming.

- Enjoy the process!

DON'T

- Doubt the process – the universe has your back!

- Give up if things don't happen as quickly as you expected.

- Miss the minor changes by only looking out for the big ones.

- Worry too much about the how and the logic of your intentions – do what you can but let the law of attraction work its magic too.

- Complain. Think of all that negative energy! (See Help! It's Not Working! on page 90 for tips on how to keep calm and carry on.)

- Try to be perfect all the time. You're only human. Remember that tomorrow is a new day.

- Expect manifestation to make sense all the time. Your logical brain will question how and why it works. Have faith.

- Ignore your gut feelings. It could well be the universe prodding you to do something.

- Spend all your time looking for signs. They will come.

Further resources

Beware — if you embrace manifestation, you'll end up down a rabbit hole of information! But it's a fascinating rabbit hole and people are incredibly happy to share their experiences. Just remember that at some point you need to stop reading and start doing!

Books

Bernstein, Gabrielle: *Super Attractor: Methods for Manifesting a Life Beyond Your Wildest Dreams*

Byrne, Rhonda: *The Secret*

Dyer, Wayne: *The Power of Intention*

Haanel, Charles F.: *The Master Key System*

Hill, Napoleon: *Think and Grow Rich*

Hurst, Katherine: *The Secret Law of Attraction: Master the Power of Intention*

King, Vex: *Good Vibes, Good Life: How Self-Love Is the Key to Unlocking Your Greatness*

Nichols, Lisa: *Abundance Now: Amplify Your Life & Achieve Prosperity Today*

Swart, Tara: *The Source: Open Your Mind, Change Your Life*

Tolle, Eckhart: *The Power of Now: A Guide to Spiritual Enlightenment*

Websites

www.thelawofattraction.com
– background to the law of attraction, visualisations, exercises and quotes.

www.sarahprout.com – articles and podcasts.

www.spritualbeing.com – practical information about the law of attraction.

www.throughthephases.com
– practical content about the law of attraction, journaling and soul care.

www.gabbybernstein.com – free resources and podcast.

My intentions

Use the space below to write down what you want to manifest. If you're not sure, just jot down notes to get your ideas flowing.

My affirmations

Use this space to write down affirmations you can use to support the manifestation process. They don't have to be set in stone and may evolve over time as you learn more about yourself.